I0417957

# JOLLY FOR NOW?

Published by Gail Mehlan/GM Sunflower Creative Arts
1155 Coral Springs Dr. Cicero, IN 46034
For more information: g.meh1974@gmail.com

Copyright © 2020, 2022 by M. M. Mehlan

All rights reserved. No part of this book may be reproduced in any
manner whatsoever without written permission except in the case of brief
quotations embodied in critical articles and reviews.

The characters and events portrayed in this book are fictitious. Any
similarity to real persons, living or dead, is coincidental and not intended
by the author.

Cover design by: M. M. Mehlan

Cataloging-in-Publication Data is on file at the Library of Congress
Printed in the United States of America

Mehlan, M. M. *Jolly For NOW?* New and Revised Edition

ISBN979-8-9866255-1-5

# JOLLY FOR NOW?

M. M. MEHLAN

GM Sunflower Creative Arts

For Edmund, and Mom and Dad
For Grandma and Grandpa Mehlan
For Grandma and Grandpa Parker
For Matt and Michelle and your families
For JM, ES, SL, CM, MM

# Contents

## IV
## I WANNA BE AN ASTRONAUT

# Introduction

Many poems are songs. Many songs are poems.
I wrote these words to make sense of difficult times,
dealing with addiction, mental illness,

loss, love, and everything in between.
I know I'm not perfect.
Some things have to be lost or forgiven.

Lost and found and lost again? Found again?
So, it goes!--It seems, in my life.

Lessons are to be learned. Myths are to be told,
and feelings are to be had.
The themes and titles of this work refer to
the *innocence* of seeing *magic* in everything.
Oh! How amazing things could be
when we were young!

Finally, upon arriving at adulthood, ashamed and perhaps almost
evil, upon abandoning this folly,
I sense the essence of being satisfied by life,
seeing the wonder in it.
For we are not broken, but instead,
perfectly our innocent selves, and that is okay. It is wonderfully okay.

--M. M. Mehlan

# I

# Rainbows and Unicorns

# Motherhood --A War

Her vehement desire stands like that of searing wrath
With penetrating eyes, swimming with fearful loss
Sadness bought and sold for too high a cost
A raging war of attrition seething inside her
The casualties too high to number
This lioness now protecting her den
FIERCE SWEAT, DRIPPING BLOOD!
Devouring the flesh of her lover's embrace
Eating his fraudulent weakness with her cold words.
CAN YOU?
Can you recite them to me?
She has buried it down six thousand miles into the
wounded flesh of her heart
Bonded in frozen iron chains, "A miracle," she whispers.
"Am I to ever love again?"
How astringent is the black?
Is this what she's held for the color of HIS sins?
Are these the sins of the father?
But, *Behold!*
She stands inflamed in *GLORY*; Now, as Master of the house,
Commander of her troops
Resolve in her glorious spirit's homecoming.

# ?(QUESTIONS)

Where is the grave in which I have buried myself?
Where is the vat in which I can drown my sorrows?
Where is the key to chains in which I have locked my heart?
Are they in the cave of sadness I have carved into my mind?
Am I bruised and broken, beyond repair?
Are my harsh words cold like swords and daggers?
Are they to be pulled from my body?
ONE? BY ONE? BY ONE?
What is the name I shall go by?
Misery, perhaps?
Is that the "ME" that I defend?
I'll try to see the journey through, the questions lost forever
Sinking deep into the impacted snow.
Is it in a rainbow in spring rains, perhaps that I will shine?
Shining bright with an everlasting glow?
I DOUBT IT........BUT?
Who knows?

# A Letter

As the sunlight peered into the window just now after dawn,
                --I never wanted to leave you.
Our son doesn't deserve a father who can't
even take care of himself.
You deserve to have a lover better than I.
Even though I know these things,
it still doesn't make my heart break any faster.
It is incredibly slow like tiny pins into flesh.
You couldn't imagine what real pain feels like.
The sinew of my bones being ripped apart by guilt.
Is it real?
Is "This" *REAL?!*
Or am I just a dead man walking in a
pair of stolen wing tip cordovan shoes?

# Prayer #1

Starting at the beginning
Pulled up by the roots
Terror at prospected sinning
If I screw up these blessings
I'll have to accept this life sentence
With wire and land mines, I'll be messing
Oh! Please, GOD! ACCEPT MY REPENTANCE.

# LOVE and Baryons for Breakfast

What is this adulthood that has sacked me?
Oh, how these computers have hacked me.
But "I'm alive," I hear as my tongue speaks
Aging less than a sack of human meat.
Liver's quite pickled in spice, a treat.
The pleasures of virtue sold out by the pound, the happiness,
I've scraped off the last of it.
I've choked it down, hacked it up, the wholly unrepentant
wrenching sound.
Bury it in the dirt, and cover it up
in fresh ice with sugar so sweet.
I've dug into the ground to plant the seeds to grow a house
but repaired it out of paste,
to break it up for who is to burn it down.

Softly--
Softly, I asked of you, "Are you feeling okay?"
The nausea has taken you down, so we sleep the hours away.
Watching TV--*Touching softly*
We spend our time saving, spending little.
"Since when did things get so costly?"
I love you. You love me. We are having a baby.
I've tucked you in every night
and cooked supper in the evenings.
I've cleaned our rooms in the mornings,

prepared but baryons for breakfast.
I washed our things in hot water.
So how clean should we be if the stain of sin were no more?
I cooked my livers in fresh oil,
for this is all that's left of our spoils.
I love you. You love me. We are having a baby.
The rain is now making me rhythms,
Feeling worse, I've seen the symptoms.
Oh! How I just want to be happy and
find the little place to call my home.
I just want to love them,
make them feel the world is in their hands.
I love you. You love me. We are having a baby.
I thought I could end the truth, assassinate it,
a two-faced halcyon of evil thoughts, the truest corruption.
The despot, the tyrannous, maligned the history
we've seen for ourselves the folly of the wise man,
How stupid the comforts we toil in this life for?
For the better part of hundred years,
the rest is but jesting and mud in our eyes,
Oh, the better part of a hundred years,
the sun will shine, and we shall see.
Greetings, Oh, posterity!
I love you. You love me. We are having a baby.
I lack time as it goes by. Who said I'm not afraid to die?
Who said I should be afraid to cry?
I wish to fly, the same as the bluebird flies
But gravity brings us down, makes us feel ashamed.
I don't want to feel this way anymore
I want to be free, free as the winds go by
Free as the summertime,
Enjoying the daylight.
I want to be free, free to dream the way babies dream,
sleeping all day long,
As free as the lullaby from momma's lips,
as we grew up way too quick,
And Time, he plays his tricks.
Free to be kind,
This love makes everything alright,

"Tell me. Is it lonely and cold down deep in the hole?
Is the moonlight a guiding sight?
I can't wait to help you out."
I love you. You love me. We are having a baby.


Awaken early to laughs, loved into a battlefield.
A plastic prophecy strewn about the kitchen
Suspicion itching at the back of my eyes
I'll trade you back the "Noes" for sighs
I love you. You loved me.
AREN'T WE having a baby?
I've left this house bones broken, heavily worn
I've cooked my dreams till burnt to hot sludge
'Til worry and sorrow came home
Did you miss me?
Pregnant stomachs like swollen feet—defeat
Is this the food that we eat?
I loved you. You loved me. I love this baby.
But it's all gone now.
Daddy's gone crazy!

# The Girls from Santiago

When you think you're escaping,
You find the longest way round is the shortest way home
But we've slain giants and seen the ghosts of old men
Who have found their way back to the start again
When love learns to love, we've learned to love, love
I wanna take ya down to the fountains of truth
So, we can bathe in the fountains of youth once again
When love learns to love, we've learned to love, love
I see our ambitions flying away
Like the pictures in the scrapbooks of our yesterday
Because my love learned to love when love was just a fool
When love learns to love, it learns to love, love
I remember the mountain air and putting flowers in your hair
Just like the girls in Santiago used to do
On our way to the oceans of many days,
We pass them through all of ourselves
So, hold fast to now
To which the future plunges through
Like an arrow straight through me, and you
Let me be who you would be
When love learned to love, it learned to love, love

# Travesty

Travesty is a word I fear
The thoughts they wrinkle and twist
Scratching the fool; footsteps
Back and forth...
Back and forth...
Swarming like chandeliers of worry
Swinging Back and forth...
Back and forth...
What shall I do? Lay myself bare?
Abandon what I feel, to find, a silent sun?
Is it a dead son or daughter?
You say we're going
The future, it seems
All and along
With it too, and down the drain
Without coming in out or down the hall
Full feeling absent in the danger
Break the siphon, Break it all
But ice, the ice
Jingles now in all the broken glass

My feet are tired, and my knees, they ache
I've slammed the door I'm left to crawl
I cannot keep the curtains open
For every fraught and thoughtless and angry notion
Still, I shake in all perceived and perpetual motion
Back and forth...
Back and forth...
Swelling oceans of endless, timeless worry
I pace...
Back and forth...
Back and forth...

# A Good Day

When early morning drunks get their fix,
they don't want to know what makes the world tick.
I'd hate to say goodbye again; I'd rather say hello to a friend.
How many dreams must I shatter today to make it a good day?
And how many lies, like tears, that I've cried
to make it a good day?
My hands are getting old; I can feel it in my bones
as I fix myself a breakfast.
The phone doesn't ring anymore as it did before,
and friends get old and move away.
How many dreams must I shatter today to make it a good day?
And how many lies, like tears, that I've cried
to make it a good day?
I know it's an old sentiment that takes my breath away
Now go away singing words while songs lament
You know I loved you only yesterday,
but never found the words to say, so I sang them.
How many dreams must I shatter today to make it a good day?
And how many lies, like tears, that I've cried
to make it a good day?
Only once, never twice, did I make a sacrifice
For a good day. For a good day, for a good day,
Let's make it a good day. Let's make it a good day.

# I Loved You First

You know I said once before, you know I'll say it again.
I know they're just words, but I'll say it again.
But you know I loved you first.
For what it's worth, I never left, but I heard, I've tried so hard,
So, I say it again, every day.
But I don't know if it's true, but I'll say it again.
I loved you first.
I see the secrets on your face; I want you to learn as I've learned.
As you get older, I see it in your bones, but I loved you first.
And I know the world. It hurts.
I throw down while you nurse.
But even though, even though while I wait.
The dream of the moment has burst.
And I hope beyond hopes that you learn just to thirst.
But remember, I loved you first.

# Sympathy for a Love Song

I sing a sad song every time I wake up.
I sing a love song, not for me, but for your sake.
I don't know if I can stand on my two feet all alone.
I'm locked inside this tomb without a telephone.
So, I can't call my friends to help me roll away my stone.
Sit back and relax. We can still get out of this place.
You look at my lips, you hoped for a kiss,
and to my surprise, we miss.
Some would say that's not up to us but up to fate.
We came into this world too late.
But we are the ones who feel the reactions,
the guilt, and pain, pleasure, and satisfaction.
The world is a stage, and we are the actors.
We choose our own player, and we play from a reaction.
Which one are you, and who am I?
Which am I to be, and how am I willing to try?

# Under the Seas of This Revolution

Painting a picture with dogs at my feet
Seeing a photograph of lost memories
I've got tears in a jar, and
I'm looking at the stars behind...Broken glass.

What happened here? I cannot say.
But I'll keep an eye out every day, with my sunglasses on.
I'm basking in the moon; I'm looking at the sun...

But under the seas of this revolution lies a lonely little boy,
Who can't figure out what he's been fighting for?
He needs resolution...
So "Jesus Christ, man! Can you help me out?"
When all I feel is this fucking doubt;
I need to understand...
And everything that's so inept at
making me feel so much regret,
I can never change.

But under the seas of this revolution
Lies a lonely little boy...
Look past these eyes, wouldn't you like to see?
Way deep down inside of me, you know time takes its toll.
Never stops by anymore to say, "Hello."

So, I went out down into the alley to look around
Thought I heard someone hanging around
But you know it's just me,
You know it's just me,
ALL Alone.

# Sylvia Rose

When Sylvia Rose puts on a show
All the boys come to see her pose
But she's dancing alone,
Watching the rows,
Waiting for her lovers to phone
But nobody knows
How lonely she is
And nobody knows
What a phony she is
When she drops you a line,
It sends chills down your spine
But when the curtain closes,
She turns up her nose
It's just when she's crying alone,
A pretty girl with no home
But she can't find any fun on her own,
You send her sympathies
When she says "Just hold me."
But you don't know she's just a phony
Where did you go, Sylvia Rose?
And what did you say,
Before you walked out the door?
What did you say to make it all ok?
To be so full of yourself
To put the past on a shelf
But you don't mind wasting my time
You think you've done
All the world some harm

Well, you've murdered yourself;
Tell me you've no friends left,
While you fool all of us with your charm
But nobody knows how lonely she is
And nobody knows what a phony she is
But when Sylvia Rose puts on a show;
All the boys come to see her pose
But she's feeling alone,
Watching the rows,
Praying for the sadness to go

# Living in the Future

It's four AM, and I can't sleep,
Why do I keep having all bad dreams?
My wristwatch a day behind
But the right time?
Working up to every moment
I'll take the abuse, hear all the white lies
I'm living in the future
I'll tell you the truth no one really knows their use
Until we're forced to choose
And I'm almost out of all good excuses
I'll tell you the truth
I'm going to share and compromise
To your surprise! I'm living in the future
One future at a time
I'm living in the future.
You'll show me yours;
I'll show you mine,
I'll trade you my memories for your time
I don't want them anymore
What good are they?
You'll show me yours; I'll show you mine
My wristwatch is a day behind
But the right time
I'm living in the future!!
I'll tell you the truth; no one really
knows what happens when you die
But if you're a lucky man,

They'll dress you in a suit and tie
Say a few good words,
All your family will cry
Is that living in the future?
I'm living in the future
Living in the future
One yesterday at a time.

# I'm a Fool!

I got a car that just don't start
I jump it just about every morning
Like a stupid fool
But it's mine, And I don't care
You know I don't sleep at night
I just don't feel alright
I get anxious and lose my cool
But you think I don't try to get sober
What really gets me stuck?
Is how you don't care
You think I'm just cruel
Yes, I'm a fool
But I'm not stupid.
I think I'm a dancing fool
You know I got all the moves
I got all the moves
I think I'm cool,
But I look stupid
I dreamed I left today
But I won't go away

I'm stuck in love,
Yes, I'm stuck in love
Yes, I'm a fool,
But I'm not stupid
I don't cry every night
But when I do,
I lose all my inhibitions
Yes, I'm a fool,
But I'm not stupid

# Empty Vessels

The wine it calls to me from the holiest of golden bottles
How can I wait to drink, to sing you songs of sorrow?
A sorrow of a song that laughs loudly
to empty vessels in my soul
The sadness, it comes as lush gardens
and streams of flowing water--
To drown the parish of joy,
the end of our joyous singing
Just as the heavens are blue,
so shall my heart be again standing tall and true
Blossoming like the tulips again in the springtime
So, tell me now, keeper of the tavern,
is your cellar full of all the golden ales?
With silent guitars and lutes ready to strike,
our cups have run dry
For these two horned things go together better
With the sweet fragrance of life
Bring us the cask and fill up my cup
Drink it down to the last drop,
for dark is this life, *dark is our death.*

# Life Makes a Sound

Dust falls down against the dirty floor
To only hear the question, ask
"What's my use?"
"What am I good for?"
But are these questions?
--Is that all?
Isn't there even something more?
You asked me, "Would You stay?"
--("Should I stay?")
Only if I believe the words she'd say
They fell like dust,
"All" has turned to dust
Damn it all, be turned to dust
Is this idea strong enough,
Is it big enough to blow it up, end it all?
I cannot leave this world in such a dirty way--
Desperate eyes
Seeking desperate words
Oh, the flash of light was as bright as day,
Has left but kind, empty shadows on the wall
The desperate sighs
In a desperate world
The cave is deeper than your thought,
So the deeper I fall
The longing you sought, desperate
Forcing me viciously to a crawl

All the while I whistle sweetly a song
You once sang to me
I only see your empty figures in the fog
Am I old enough to just give up?
On this world I'm in?
OH! In this world, I'm stuck
Tell me, has there been enough time?

# The Killer

The walls are closing in on me now. I can't breathe
They said if I just said I'm sorry, they'd set me free
But instead, I'll plead guilty,
And they'll take my life away from me
But they caught me red-handed,
Tonight, I'll be branded, reprimanded
Then taken to the Yard!
I'll tell you it was worth it.
I can see who you are in the mirror
Now I know I'm the man they say I am.
I feed off that fear
I can see how deep it can go,
My conscience is clear
I sent the mad kings to Valhalla
Because they ate my sons and daughters
But now their screams have left me violent and cold
In the night, I'll be beaten at random
And be left to die all alone
Because I tried to build a place, I called IT
"Home"

# Headache #1

Pounding blisters into the back of my spine,
A sugared pulse of pain
Strain in my ignorance
Temperance has led to spastic interceptions
Of necessary brain-trained responses
Sweet liquor of the attention deficit dispensers
Brewed mind aches of lost mood enhancers

# Headache #2

Bang! Smack! Slap!
BOOM! BOOM! BOOM!
Doomed at the end of a rope
Choking down the sweet strokes of harsh, blinding obliteration
Doomed to sleepless hardship, pulsating joints
Divining rough considerations
Last resorts of my thoughts tender less suffocation

# Dry

Tepid air for empty rooms
The smoky smell clears out the gloom
The sticky turns to dry when the world of words
closes in on the one
Soon.
At once, the morning forest of reflections
had meditated on dreaded regret
The impending calamity the only mantra
known as ticking clocks hands click
A solemn tune
Soon.
Soon.

# Hunger

Hunger like a dog
Hungry and potent feed for the hogs

Digging sweet things into the muck and mud
Praying for pity in empty troughs
Burning down these paper walls
Wailing mares in the sight of studs

Hunger down into the pits
Hungry deep a wrenching stomach stitch

Eating feasts with starving paupers
Cooking peas in laundry soup
Turning glazed eyes into sticky goop
Leaning into oiled kettle stirs

Hunger to stave off the burning souls
Hungry to score the winning goal

Craving gold for these swollen bellies
Rising dough for lusts licking lips

Hunger be gone on shrinking hips
Hunger be gone while drinking sweet shining drips-
*Drip- Drip- Drip-*

# Pills

I do not wish to take these pills
I thought I was sad, moving by others' wills
I fear the medicine is making me ill
I had amassed the confidence, but now giving me chills
I really don't trust 'em, Doc, these colorful pills.
I do not wish to do what the colorful pills will.

# Guitar

Following the lines to
The curve of her spine
Her hips telling me
Lies in forgotten crevasses
"She is mine."
Oh, "Now kisses must be earned.", she says
Time has worn her
Time is tired
Time loses its soft meticulous touch
"Kisses, my boy, must be earned."
Lateral space opens between my ears,
Melodies in dark temples fill the empty halls
Each scar worn a little deeper than the next
Soft tissue between her ribs and thighs
My fingers can only now softly touch
Flowers blooming in her harmonious eyes
Screaming in pleasure, shivering nights
Only now, while gently playing

# Precious Flowers

--Porous futures--Ripping sutures--Precious flowers
Sweet stinging, sorrow of pain
That radiates like the sun
Over the frost November Sunday
The pain of hearts lasting into nights
Filled with passionate sweat
Trading adequacy for efficiency
Love for lost layers of flesh pound for pound
Hammering petals on hardwood tables
Beauties withering sweetness
Fading shades of color
Lost days and past memories
Honeyed laboring September weakness
Longing lusts of lofty singing tomorrows--Beckoning

# Grace

Sweet words among strangers
Once familiar dangers gone
Who were we when the curtains opened?
When the face and masks had boiled over?
"I knew you once."
I said in my mind
"You knew me too."
The response to myself was not kindly omitted
Who can feel the ghost of your breath in my ears?
As a sweet "I love you" falls silently dead
Glittering flakes peeled off a colorless world
A faint sparkle shining bright in the iris of confident stares
None have had your lovers embrace
But I've felt your soft, harmless hands
A long reach of hopes amending "Grace."

# The Cracks

I built it up strong once
A fanciful presence, glistening concrete
Every tiny crack begins to show
How do people forget?
"Sticks and stones," they said
"Never broke my bones!"
But the cause of tiny cracks begins to rupture
A serving full of suffering means,
Slop!

I had wiped the slate clean once
Cleared the air of the stinking shit
If people knew the strength, I'd had
Maybe they could take a share, one or two
If you feel like I do, maybe you'd care
How do people forget?

Shades of a sober temperament
How long have I suffered in pain in darkness?
Through angry "spirits" and drunken teardrops
It came in calm winds through red-headed beauties
Laughing through the broken hearts
Fair-skinned brilliance through hard work and earned duties
How do people forget?

Tell me I was good once, vying for truth, muscles burned hard
Searching for waters in fountains, turned off

Home was where the heart died, beating its last,
On the bloodied cutting board
Every twitching wince a lie of new life.
Tribulation masked in your deep suffering breaths

In public, I tried putting on the charm,
But my lack of enthusiasm should have rung alarms
Music rang out to silence as I searched
To find the veins in my arms
Blinded by exquisite suffering, ended
Oblivion felt as sweet dripping nirvana
I remember it all, the roaring serf,
Before it falls, relief.
I remember it all...

# The Ballad of Jolly and Sylvia

**Part 1**

Tell me your sins, Jolly, tell me your crime.
Do you remember?
Her laughter was contentious, but she could spit on a dime
Her sex was explosive, her beauty to be committed, like a crime
I tell myself these words and desire the truth, but conscience is
hard when covered in slime

"Tell me something, sweet Sylvia. I know I can make you mine."

"Take it, easy little boy, love will come soon, but It will
take some time."

The wait is hard when feelings are true,
I'm Jolly for now, but my sadness is the only tune
I remember you there at the brass bar, attraction brewed
Sipping scotch, reading the bards of old news
The portrait is mine of the Dorian kind, which glared
A rotten man now hangs in the attic, and it's not fair
These were the prophecies of a great and mysterious adventure
I never intended the muses to send us out into this.
This terrible life: now I wish to mend her

"Sylvia, OH SYLVIA, oh Sylvia Rose, where did you go?"

--I could hear Sylvia speak; from far off in the dusk--

"I never left you, my boy; you've broken my trust
I've built a wall around myself to protect me; I must."

I began speaking to myself, thrashing the ground, throwing
them now, handfuls of dust--

"Oh Sylvia, Sylvia, I'm begging you, please, tell me you love me.
I'm down on my knees; I cannot bear this travel;
it's too far. I cannot climb your wall; I'm far across the seas
They rise, and they fall; if they froze in the winter,
I could skate across them all
But my knees have become shaky, and the time is untrue,
Please, oh Sylvia, I'm destined to fall."

--Sylvia's whispers now drowning the sorrow
down deep into my core--

"You know how to love; you did once before.
Just be yourself, and I'll open the door."

**Part 2**

"Sign my appeal! Oh, lady, that the muses remind me of a past
that has risen before;
An apparition that defies my logic long before I lost sight of land.
This, oh you, my Lady Macbeth!
That madness hath changed us for yesterday, oh!
Yesterday is happiness but a dream?
We sing! We sing!"


Yesterday was supposed to be the happiest day of our lives
But instead, we both are tired and filled with
empty thoughts and tries
Sticky toys and while tripping through the night
scrambling to ease baby's cries
We traded flowing gowns and matching vests
For inverted frowns and molded plastic toy T-rex
For daisies and wedding bells still seeped into my bright dreams
After putting all the family to bed and shutting down
my mind's terrible screams
I pictured you smiling through late fall showers
and harvest moonlit beams
We left our friends there, in an alternate life,
waiting for us to arrive
But instead, we left them waiting too long,
so we could just survive
But what a life would that have been?
Without breaking our bones sweeping up late,
at bars and arcades,
for toy cars and Fourth of July parades
For early morning hugs and tired sighs for smiles
that never cease from the gibberish plays,
crab night dinners and perhaps games with no winners
If we weren't so tired, it would not be just out of our sight
I wouldn't trade how I feel for knowing we did one thing right.
For all the mistakes and late-night sighs
If we weren't so tired,
I'd say we've arrived at the happiest days of our lives
"Sylvia, can you hear and respond to my thoughts?"

--But I only hear them as sighs--

"Yesterday is gone, my little boy; you destroyed the magic of joy.
Have I not suffered enough, or is suffering your ploy?
Are you mistaken, or has the loneliness
left you hopeless and paranoid?"

"Torture me no more, Sylvia, please!!
I'm Jolly, for now, burning in this hell I've enjoyed."

"It isn't I who is torturing; you've paid your ferryman
across the river of sorrow.
You can find your way back; it's all in the plan;
you can save your own soul if you try
You're loved in the land of the living; you're needed in time,
you're needed now, for you are the strength of the heart,
my boy, just follow the golden silk of joy
It will lead you to the ruins of the home you've destroyed."

As Sylvia's voice began to fade, the sun now gone
I began reflecting on what we used to call home
Home--am--I--all alone?
Small spaces encased in glass
I've picked it up; I'm ready to smash
The futures are gone
Have my shaken hands turned to a plastic stone
Am I all alone? Is there no place that I can call home?
Home was where I dried my shoes
Where we worshiped the electric firelight
Where love was supposed to abide and survive
But I've been blinded by bright cathode-ray tubes
A soft whisper betrays,

    "I feel used."

    "Me too."

**Part 3**

Has loneliness come to shelter in the home of my heart?
Has the lonely muse given advice not yet taken?
I cannot see into your crystal ball; the tarot has not yet spoken
The future has yet to be written, but the past is worn into
the stone now weathered
Bitter is its sting.

"Who are you, Jolly? What are your sins?"

"I'm Jolly for now, but who have I been?"

"Tell me your sins, boy; the judgment is true."

"I lost the fight to Sadness, a Dragon.
I don't know where to begin."

"Your excuses have become tiresome,
your weakness shining through."

The dragon approached me one fine and gruesome day
In a forest of thistles that had pulled me away
His eyes were piercing like that of a sword
I wanted to save my sweet princess, her love, my reward
But the dragon had torn me and swallowed me whole
And sweet Sylvia was scared he'd eaten my soul
But I pulled out my dagger, my sensational pride
To rid myself of these vermin, a desolate plight
This dragon now speaking, a whispering thunder,
Oh! Such a gruesome terrible fright.

"Your prince is a liar; his weapons rusted through
His endless permissions to himself are for you."

"Sweet Sylvia! Oh, Sylvia! The dragon is right
He's taken my heart and ended the fight."

The corpses lay wretched on silvery tombs

As a battle of wits was fought in this wintery gloom
A man has lost solemnly; his mortality sewn
Into great fissures of madness that his brutal hands had hewn
The death of this dragon as he breathed his last breaths.

"You've taken my life, but I've taken your sight
You cannot see the ones whom you love, and I'll ruin your life
You'll dream of their warmth for loneliness and strife,
now end it quickly, sweet prince, now pull out the knife."

"Careful"

"Pull the dagger out slowly--
Its dull edges tearing in
The burst of joy into the syringe
Shedding crimson tears
It only takes one
To feel the cold restless fears
You know where you've been
You've taken the bruises
From the place that you stand
Clenched fists, open hand
Pull my spirits from the empty crushed cans
Drawn out like a loose thread
Tapping truths out of the lies in your head
Twisting steel girders manufactured
Of things that were said
Cheat me out of goodness done
Making way for sorrow won
Empathy now loaded into chambers
Of my sympathy gun."

The words on my lips screamed out at this terrible errand.

"Now die, you sweet evil-born dragon;
it's Jolly whose strength was--
It's Jolly who's won!"

**Part 4**

"My princess is gone, the fields full of thorns
I remember this place that sunflowers adorned
It was beautiful once, a garden maintained
There was a lake full of beauty, but it's dried up,
and only sand remains."

"Jolly, my boy, where are you going? There's dragon's blood
on your hands, and you're trying to wash them in sand."

"I'm Jolly, for now, but I can't get clean; it stains my skin,
and there's a curse on the land.
Oh, take away this feeling! I can't let it win;
take it away forever; I'll be scrubbing my hands."

The dawdling cat that followed me now, his golden fur
glinting in the old gray sun
He was carousing with the mice; he would play with them,
let them free, and let them run
His balance not wavered; he was on the prowl,
a predator's dance. I could see what good fun
The cat's wandering words now emptying out sour,
with sarcastic and opulent, radiant puns.

"This land has been cursed; it's falling apart
All the people have forgotten how to plant in the earth,
it used to be a paradise, and I call it "The Worth.""

"The Worth was the place where the muses would play;
they'd dance around naked,
amusing the youth when music and picture had wonderful use."

"Why do you tell me these stories of The Worth?
I've defeated the dragon, the scourge of my earth,
I remember this place from long ago;
I drew from it all that bemused. I spent many hours dancing to
the music and watching the beauty of the sunrises and sets,
many days with gorgeous women in the days of my youth."

"Sylvia's been here; we had played in this land,
it's where I gave her a ring on the finger of her left hand
She was my woman, and I was her man. But those days are lost
and buried down in the tombs of
this land you call The Worth."

"Don't suffer my conscience, you feline defiler;
you're the sorcerer here and the source of its mirth,
why don't you let your stranglehold free in vibrancy demand?
I just wish for Sylvia to see the growth in this land;
I'll plant a good seed
in the bowels of the earth, and it'll grow and grow
and bring beauty to our Worth."

"But, lo!" The cat said.

"JOLLY! An army approaches their banner held high;
the trumpets are issuing shards by the hour."

So, I followed him now to the base of the hill. The smell in the air
of a thousand deceased turned sour.

"A battle is raging just above the next hill, so guide me,
young kitten, to the commander in charge.
I wish to issue him orders before the infantry march.
I can hear them calling; I can almost make out the sound,
I'll scream at the past till I'm dead in the ground."

The cat now screamed a terrible scream breaking
my conscience and ending the scene
And began to recite the memories of friendships
lost in battles and dream.

"Don't go. It's a trap,
fighting the ghosts of the past.
They cannot die hard for they lived, and they
died and are seeking their rest."
<<<<<<<<<<<<<<<<<<<(((((((((((***))))))))))))>>>>>>>>>>>>>>>>>>>

Where do we stand if not on uneven ground?
Have we suffered ashes to dust, paid flesh by the pound
Swallowed deep in our suffering, now living in burial mounds
If the sugar were real, it wouldn't be so bittersweet
But we've been trampled beyond the
headwind by deadly defeat
Tired, miserable smoke cleared as
The rank smell of dying fleshy meat
Of the guarded bulkhead, don't blame my men
for this mess; they retreat
My slowly sinking spirit protects me
with the cavalry behind
A sea of wounded and almost dying,
they've peeled off our flanks like orange, and its rind
We'll die in these trenches if you
don't send my word to the Kind
My best friend is dying
His corpse right beside me
I tell him he's fine
BUT ALL HAS BEEN LOST
Now, we're broken
We're crying
I opened my mouth and ended the dream, and
what came out was truth, or so it would seem.

"But I'm Jolly for now, and I don't need to carry
the trembling words, their lives on my back I can't,
it's absurd: I only wished to plant courage
in the soil of the Worth, and now a battle rages for a right
to this turf, I remember this place full of daisies,
flowers, flowing with wine, now its tallow and
mud, laid with the rotten corpses divine,
it was Jolly's here once; now it's food for the swine."

"Did you forget something useful Jolly?
I'm a feline for now, but they used to call me Elijah and
Osiris before that, I may be a cat, but oh, I'm so much more than that."

## Part 5

"I was there before you were born.
I'll be there when they weigh your heart
I may not make my presence known but
you and me; we've never been far apart
I was beside you moving your hand way
before you were in dragon-infested lands
I was there when joy would move
your parts and make you dance
I was the one who gave you, yes you, another chance
I moved the tides from high to low
I made you special, and this you should know
I know I made you feel much stronger than most
But I was your mover, your holy ghost
I was there watching when you pulled Sylvia close
And told her you'd love her better than those
I was the one who gave you your child
I will be there for him, too, if he's wild like you
I was the purpose; I was your point
I was your maker
I can tell you it's true
You called me Lord, and I called you son
But you're Jolly for now, and your games are no fun
Your burden is heavy; now, pull off that yoke.
You say you're Jolly for now, but no one laughs at your jokes
You forgot me before
You'll forget me again
In the darkness, you'll ask me and say it in prose
When you want to be free, no longer tied like a dog to a post
You'll remember me, Jolly, when you pull your loved ones in close
Because I am the one who loves you the MOST."

"I'm Jolly, for now, and I see that it's true,
then why do you follow me as this obstinate cat?
I feel like I'm walking, falling into a trap
I know what IS righteous
I know that it's you."

"The Judges are coming; I can smell their burning fumes,
Now tell me, oh, feline, now what do I do?
I don't have my weapons; I only have my mind;
I must fight these old judgments
If I only had a sword, a sword from that land,
the Land of the Kind."

"You're worthless; you're ugly, you've found no good use,
you have nothing to offer us, so take our abuse."

"I could hear it forever; I've heard it before the Judges,
the rotten, now singing their tune."

"I can see them approaching. I could run them all through,
But what? Is that Sylvia?
I know it's a lie!! It mustn't! It can't!! Tell me it's untrue,
tell me, oh, tell me she isn't one of you!!!!"

**Part 6**

"OH! SYLVIA, OH! SYLVIA, SYLVIA, NO!!!!"

"Jolly, I'm here, it is but a farce, and I've been talking to our son,
and this one is the cat
I'll love you forever; I don't have a choice,
people say what they will, but I'll use my own voice
But you've had a choice and used your voice,
you've locked me in the tower, Jolly,
you put me away, but I was not one of your books
to be pulled out on a rainy day
I'm surprised at you, Jolly. You seem to know what to do,
we parted our ways, but our son, he's the glue
You know that my favorite color is blue, but I don't want
to feel it painted in truth,
Do you??
But keep fighting the battle, Jolly for now,
and maybe someday these walls will come down,
and the weight of this love will be of some use,
but now, you old joker, you can do it alone,
keep fighting the battle. I'll come around,
but stop kidding yourself,
you and I know you're no clown!
If you love me, I'll see it, look into the mirror
to see you're a father, now be it!!
I can be kind to you, Jolly. I can hand you the sword,
now destroy these old Judges and fill in the void.
They cannot destroy you. They seem only to leave you
anxious and annoyed
But remember, Jolly, remember our boy,
you were there at his birth,
now show him you're king, the king of your Worth,
show him the Judges won't penetrate your mind and
strike down this thinking with the sword from the Kind.
Jolly, I know that it's hard; I accept that you sinned, but
just take off that makeup and let go
And just try to move with it, the wind."

BUT!! BUT...
Why don't I feel whole?
There's an empty space between my skin and my soul
I just don't want to feel this way anymore
As if living has lost its luster, leaving only
embers burning deep in my core
I'd rather feel guilty than the ever-angry shame
I listen to the thoughts, and they come out
mangled and maimed
Worn down and rust sanded by the highest grain
I know it can never be the same
DULL!! BORED!! TIRED!! Asleep
The depression is old, and the wound is too deep
The words all seem useless, and adjectives cheap
I wish I could grasp at what seems out of reach
It's up there sitting, just on the top shelf
But I can't seem to stand; when I've cut out myself.

"JOLLY, OH, JOLLY! Jolly, for now, pull off that mask
and stop being a clown
We'll get there; we'll get there; now turn your face upside down."

So, give me desperate sleep
I cannot stand the pressure
You've shoveled concrete and rebar in my bones,
lapping up the pain like a thirsty dog
Weighed down, my muscles bent thick
wading through Sylvia's words like a bog
Will liberty bare her luscious tits for suckling babes
thirsting for precious "drops?"
Anchored now low in retreat where
anger begins, and the regression stops
Laughing so loudly, I plant the silent madness "crops."
And harvest will come at the end when the reaping is
left in the hand of a master, death's tangled "knots."
Please stop cooking my frigid feelings,
turning them to flowing water
in empty swollen "pots."
The thought starts ripping my heart out of this mess,

Power from the chest
Returning richness to the soil
From the rotting fruit, freshness to spoiled.

"Sylvia, Oh, Sylvia!
I know that you've gone."

So Jolly, for now, will plant again this season and continue his toil
A feather, it falls
Just now, it caught me in silence
Just now, the words soft, like my mother's
As I got ready to start again pushing the plow
To show that Jolly is good and he knows how.

"Jolly?
Do you remember long ago?
When you were just a few years old
When the land was full of wizards, fairies,
buried treasures, and gold?
Remember the day when it stopped,
and all you heard was 'Do what you're told.'"
What, then, did you find when the nights
were scary and cold?
You came out a little different, I know,
so that is why they had broken the mold
And the weight became too heavy for you,
so you hid it in the fold
That little secret place,
Your own little space,
That child, he lives,
He remembers the wizards, the fairies,
buried treasures, and gold
There's power in that place
That no one can hold."

**Part 7**

"I've never felt so lost before."
That line is not the hello that this mind described
I find an ole' Gideon but,
I just sit here in hopes that it speaks to me.
But, oh, how silent words say nothing
They appear as but strange symbols
Pressed deep on the page
Unsavory life, for once, was the hardest
is but now, pressed for sleep.
It's all I know.
A week gone, a day, perhaps
It's but prolonged agony
She came upon me like a forlorn Tinkerbell,
The Queen of Fairies, "Would you like to join
me on this journey?"

"Of course," I said. "It's only just me and this
old cat."

"Well, I'm Jolly, for now? These are my sins.
So, you know who this traveling clown is and
maybe we can be off again."

"Well," I said, "Come on, let's go!"

We found ourselves at the corner of a castle, this
seems like good work.

"We'll make it our home, and the little boy can come
and visit you here."

It was a happy home for a year and a day.
But lo! The "Things"
The new Monster of old had heard of "Jolly for now."
He knew he was in a new land
But this time, they came without trumpets blaring.

"We came at the 'hest of your Queen Fairy, your love."

Our friend, the cat, began to chuckle.

"Oh, my dearest, oldest friend, you thought she could
replace me. When all the while, she was merely the
Princess of Cleves. She was Delilah, ready to cut your hair.
She loved you and the boy as long as you had the dragon's
gold left to give her."

"No!" I exclaimed. "This can't be true.

First, it was Sylvia; now it's you?"

"You've always had me." Purring, this old cat.

The Things
they come, then they go
they eat the dead, they spoil the soul

"So, pick up the sword, Jolly. You remember the fight?"

"But, I left it in the coils of the dragon, buried deep in his bones."

"This may be true," said the cat.
"But it's the only way to defeat *The Things*. Then perhaps sing.
"The vanquished lives of the Things."

So off we went, me and the cat. Back to the trail, we went to
try to find the bones of the dragon we had once killed.
Back through the wastes, back through the thick,
to find the bones were a terrible sight.
The smell of wretch and maggots filled the air.
But to my surprise and the surprise of the cat--the sword was gone!
Taken--
    Stolen--
        Lost beyond despair--

# Walking Away

If there's something more painful than walking away
Walking away from the ones you love
I do not want to know how that feels
For this is the feeling of burning at the stake
If the smoke had not killed you first
This is the feeling of drowning at sea
If you're stranded and do not die of thirst
This is the rock that is unmovable
In the pit of your guts
This is the cold you feel before the warm drip
Of first blood
This is the feeling of walking away
Walking away from the ones you love

# Unrelenting Joy

Growing Smiles
Hugging hands
Each day stretches on forever
without seeing your learning face
"Wow, how big you've grown."
I'll say, "What a glorious day!"
I will not miss another moment
Love will find its way in
un-avoided crushing torrents
Growing smiles,
Hugging hands
Time is but slowly passing,
the drop of single grains of sand
The journey has been hard
in these harsh and empty lands
I pray for dreams of unrelenting joy
For just one embrace from my son
The little boy--

# I Love You

I should have seen the omens
I should have seen the problem
But I couldn't stop the avalanche
But now I take a stance
I'll take a chance
I love you
     I love you
          I love you
               I love you
                              I love you

   I love you
      I love you
I love you     I love you
          I love you
             I love you
               I love you
                   I love you

I love you
            I love you
I love you
I love you
                    I love you

I love you
   I love you
      I love you
        I love you
I love you
                    I love you

I love you
  I love you

                I love you
                  I love you
                    I love you

I love you

              I love you

I love you
I love you

                      I love you

I love you
    I love you
        I love you
          I love you
I love you

                      I love you

I love you
  I love you

                I love you
                  I love you
                    I love you

I love you

              I love you

I love you
I love you

                      I love you

I love you
  I love you

                I love you
                  I love you
                    I love you

I love you

              I love you

I love you
I love you

                      I love you

I love you
    I love you
        I love you

 I love you
I love you
 I love you
I love you
 I love you
 I love you I love you
 I love you
 I love you
 I love you
I love you
 I love you
I love you
I love you
 I love you
 I love you
 I love you
 I love you
 I love you
 I love you
 I love you
 I love you
 I love you
 I love you
 I love you
 I love you
 I love you I love you I love you I love you
 I love you.
 I love you
 I love you
I love you. I love you
 I love you
 I love you I love you
I love you

I'll say it a hundred times
It doesn't mean what it did

# Grandpa's Smile

I haven't seen you in twenty years
maybe I inherited all your fears
I remember saying,
"Grandpa, come, let's have some fun."
"Gail, come get your son."
To you, I was just a child
maybe just a little too wild
your blood runs thick through
me and you, I can't escape it
the feelings subdued
I never thought I'd live up to you
But I look in the mirror
I can barely remember that wild child

# Monsters

I'd be remiss
If I said there are no monsters
There are
And they're us
We all have it in us
I'm not here to say we are
But we could be
I do not believe in the good or evil
BUT OF MOLDED CLAY VESSELS
Some are full of wonderful things
Unicorns and Rainbows
Others filled with rot and muck
Some are crushed under the pressure
Others are built strong
Some are weak and fissure
And some need to be discarded
The beautiful vessels
Filled with garbage
Are the worst of the lot.
These will be the means
Of our impending doom
Whether by neglect or accident
Perhaps by ignorance
They know the role they play
But the world could be ours

Now see what fills your vessels
Look into it really deep--
As deep as you can look
And make sure
You're not hiding a monster

# Can You Feel It 2?

We only get to experience perfection for a moment
Before it's gone--for it's like something sweet
Like a fruit that's gone rotten
As if my hands are always shaking
For my body's endless aching
Tell me why--I don't understand the pain that's real
I know you can feel it 2
Can you feel it 2?
Cause we used to be in love
We used to share our souls above
We wanted to grow old together--but it's gone
But we couldn't stand this stormy weather alone
I played this guitar till my fingers bled
I wept into my hands till the tears had turned red
I thought if the universe had a plan, it would have
Taken It's time to breathe out its good intentions
But I don't think the good things are worth the mention
I know you can feel it 2
It's like we used to be in love

# The Septet

**I (1.)**

I am good
I am at peace
I know myself
I am aware of my surroundings
I am moving even though I am still
I know my thoughts, but my path is not set by them
I know my actions, am willing to change, moving to right actions
I know the objects set forth before me
I know the obstacles in my path
I will not be stopped, only diverted
I am a cause
I think about good intentions
I am fully aware of my body, my brain, and my soul-
These are not illusions

**II (2.)**

Be able to see past the illusions
They can be blinding
Give yourself the freedom to believe (everything and nothing)
Taking what is true and piecing it together through patience and humility
Know the reality
Acknowledge the lies
Making it a discernment
Choosing for yourself, your own path
Forgive anyone and everyone who has wronged you
No matter how serious the offense
Anger and strife are the cause for a lack of understanding

We feel it in our bodies, environment, and soul
We must be aware of these and sacrifice our emotions for the settling of
the mind
We must find the source of forgiveness
Forgiveness is the fruit of the world and our ultimate peace

### III (3.)

Love one another and banish hate from your mind
Hate builds up no family for support
No one can carry the burden alone
I know what I feel
I know how to feel
I have knowledge of my range in emotions and
    know how to use them
I will not use my emotions as a weapon
    against my friends or enemies
I will not use my emotions as an excuse for my actions
    BUT I WILL FEEL STRONGLY
Empathy, sympathy, compassion, and mercy
Grace for grace; person to person

### IV (4.)

Are you afraid?
What or whom are you afraid of?
Knowing will help overcome this fear
The simplest answer is usually the correct one
But may not be the most obvious
I will make a change
To not live in fear
Even of death for which is my end
Are you hungry? Have something to eat
Are you angry? Resolve the conflict
Are you lonely? Find a friend
Are you tired? Have a rest
These will lead to fear.
We must find the end of it.

### V (5.)

Are you an animal?
You are!!!
When your basic needs are not met
This drives the mind to deviant- criminal- destructive behavior
Take care of yourself
Eat and drink, walk and move
Clean yourself--
Clean body
Clean thoughts
Clean clothes
Clean world
Now allow yourself to be more than the animal
Do not give in to the cravings that destroy you
Use your mind when your body is taken care of
YOU CAN

### VI (6.)

Music and art are good
They must be learned, practiced, and part of your everyday
Part of your living
I will dance
I will sing
I will play the rhythms I feel, and I know
I will be disciplined and feel their vibration
I will show these things to be true
I will observe the colors I see
For I can only see this small portion of reality
But I must be aware and in its presence
Then it will flow out of me
Create because I can
It is in me, and I will not deny this of myself
I know I can be more

## VII (7.)

Love and be loved
Solitude traps my soul in a burden of anguish
Sadness cannot be relinquished from my mind alone
For warmth and hospitality, and kindness builds up a strong family
It allows for a sense of community to rise
Receive with gladness all good things
Expect nothing from mistrust
Give all that you are able
Blood sweat, and tears for good
Expect nothing in return
And love will find you in abundance
Love is the most you can give
And once you give it
Those that have it can get nothing more from you
It is the greatest gift

I may not be a model man, but I know in my mind how;
goals must be set and mantras must abide.
Words have been kind to me lately.

# Words

Words are like weapons, some are light, some are heavy,
some are sharp, some dull, but the damage they do,
well, that depends on how you wield them.
But make sure you know how to use them
correctly or you might just lose one of your own fingers.

# Dread

It's pretty much all I feel these days.
Why? Don't know, But it's there,
*Looming.*

# The End #1

The end is only the beginning of the future
The future is only hope until the end
I hope to see you again my friends
When I send you my regards from the land of the living
And if you see me on the other side
Send me home and hope again
To see the pictures of your face
I will make you laugh, and cry tears of wondrous joy
In the end I'll see you there to make us all brand new

# II

# I Just Might be the Devil

# My Sweet Queen Marie

My sweet queen Marie,
The dead man's spirits lay beneath the tree
The light of rebirth out sadness sweet as fresh potted earth
I came to see what light I could bear
to build you up as a good and holy mother of all
and sweet queen to the lost
Oh, now my sweet queen Marie,
The story told by magi, prophets, and bards of old,
a story of love that could have been
a knight whose armor was wearing thin
You took him made him a consort and he raised you up
and the children you bore had a lot in this house
For soiled masking of searing coals,
it needs too quick by demons so bold
The choices you made last, could be better
You lost in your mind the battle won by your soul
But I was the warrior who fought for your time
And too lush were the words of the serpent that you now know.
Who would?
The evil took my home, took my children broke my pride,
bruising my spirit deep on the inside
I turned the other cheek and then I let it bleed me
For I will rise like a fireball and
defeat the evil with my flames set apart
A fiery sword to guardian angels seeking the light
You've taken my sweet queen Marie
The sums ruffled all up with your lies
You destroyer of goodness you destroyer of homes

The monster of misfortunes being restlessly sworn
Where did you go my lover, my friend?
The serpent has taken your mind, repent!!
We've opened Pandora's Box
A wrath of rebukes, a parasitic sentimental pride
Shame on you for your fruitless ways,
your children buried in a pit of your own destruction,
shame on you for cauldrons of love spilled out for fanciful whims,
desires never fulfilled searching for the dead in empty tombs
Let them lie open for yours this demeaning prostitution
When a ring of trust was offered for less than suffering
Shame on you for the devil's pride,
for breaking the yokes of honesty
The demons roar and the universe split
Who is responsible for this game?
Rebuked for evil done to friends
In search of lust and love unchained
For in sultry lattices, you birthed nothing but shame,
And this unholy unquenchable pain
But lo, the bidding of hearts be damned
I wish only for a night I could hold you in my arms
and tell you everything will be alright
and things will be so much better;
to see the smile you make when the warmth
of lovemaking, has made you happy
to hear the muffled sighs and snores of satisfaction
in your sleep to rub your arms with my strong hands
as you lay quiet in peaceful joy
To clear the air with sage and myrrh so the shadows
don't disturb our rest in peaceful dreams
of enlightened hope in a house filled with calm.
Just for one more night could I be your rock and your strength,
Just for one night could I see you truly at rest
just for one night, we could be as calm as the sea
But fates be damned this night may never be
This knight has laid down his sword
He shakes in never-ending dying strokes
His side has been pierced just like our Lord's, a savior he is not,
perhaps a martyr for a whore

Into the great wilderness, he goes,
alone and in darkness, his armor still worn
I cannot now save you from the death that you own,
but life has a way of getting me home
This isn't a future of possible lives,
but a symphony of destruction of possible pasts.

# The Battle

I will fight!!!
I will never lay down my sword!!!
Even though this armor is worn and
my soul is sullenly dressed as if it wore garments,
It was torn
I will fight for love
I will fight for forever
I will never stand to be
The one who's ripped to the ground
A corpse is but only a rotten thing
A pulse it beats, while still alive
I love you to the
Ends of the universe
Where dark mysteries
Lie for us to discover
This war will never desist
Till I see your face reborn,
The silent sadness be lost
And can never think to return
I am a knight
Fighting--For your all,
All that is desired by your love
I am a knight in the
Shaman's dance
Placid darkness,
Cold, constant turmoil
As the crimson blood
Flings from my sword

For this--
For this--
I may not be strong enough
I may not be bold enough
But in my silence,
Deep in every corner of my heart
I love you.

# I Just Might be the Devil--Part 1

As she rolled over sweat still dripping
Radiating with quaint shivers of pulsating
Electric ecstasy "You just might be the devil."
She said, "I think I need to repent."
She thinks, it's only fun
But I want to touch her soul
I gave her all my energy
And now this moment, I'm spent
You'll never know how I feel
I thought
"You don't love me like I love you. No, you don't.
I just might be the devil." I said
"But you must be a witch."
You put a spell on me with your eyes
And I know you will break my heart
It'll end with wailing cries
We both now lay together in absent satisfied sighs
Slightly touching a clasp on her inner thighs
If I was the devil, I'd never listen to your succulent lies;
I'd know that nothing would ever be a satisfactory surprise.
"But you don't love me like I love you. No, you don't."
I've done everything to you in a million lifetimes
In a million ways, in a million universes, a million times
I've said I love you, and a million times
You've responded in kind, but you're not mine

I've broken you down and broken your heart
I've made you happy and given you tenderness and joy
I've given you every atom of my being
And our minds have melted together
Perhaps one day I'll see
And the traps of flesh will set us free
You've done the same to me
A million times
Perhaps I was created to fall forever--
Just like my dearest friend the devil
Fall and fall and fall over and over again
In and out of your presence
I just might be the devil
I just might need to be in your glory of gods
But perhaps your life suffices
"Perhaps I can never have you."
And I've offered up this damned thing as a sacrifice
And damned forever in your pit
A flaming river of despair
I just might be the devil
Perhaps what is broken can never ever be repaired
I believed you when you said you loved me
And now that was only the present then,
But it is not the present now
But I believe it still might be true, a million different ways
In a million different worlds, while a million different times
We've shared some words of truth
Or perhaps I'm the father of lies
Perhaps I've exhausted my resources
At least I've tried.

# Off the Bed

I remember a dream you had
Wedding bells, perhaps a happy scene
Was it simply that these thoughts made you glad?
Or was there another running theme?
Blank eyes tied to the bedpost, the bluest of sad
Sweeping the gentle remains of our love
Off the bed.
Could we run away from this life,
Pretend perhaps that we are the dead?
Could it be like all the love stories I've read?
Could I steal you away from yourself
And all the empty nights lost in your head?
Could I have all the things back that you once said?
Please take my hand
Place a ring where your finger commands
Maybe it's a promise to mend a broken heart
Like we had planned, but I'm not sure
If I can watch you walk away again
Sweeping the gentle remains of our love
Off the bed.

# The Drops--

It's a simple dilemma
My heart is just too big
And it pushes out my insides
Squeezing out my essence
Just there to the corners of my eyes where--
The little drops, they form
Just before gravity makes them rain down onto my hands--
Sometimes I wipe them away with my fingers
Just to save them
The hard fall that they have to take to reach there
But--
They always end up just where they're meant to be
Until on a hard day when my heart grows
        and grows and squeezes more drops out of me
The drops fall down to the ground and
        go down into the earth and down to the ocean and then
Up into the sky and then they
        -rain -down -on -me and I fill my hands
Drink them up, *Perhaps the heavens cry,* I thought--
"*Because the heart of the world is just too big to...*"
"Like me?" A voice then whispered--
        sounding so far away
Just as the rain began to slow--
"Be calm, save your drops, I have enough of mine to share."

# I Just Might be the
# Devil--Part II

She arose off of me into a cloud of sheets
Cigarette smoke dancing in the air
And we haven't got a care at all
I can feel your desire, sweet girl--But you don't love me
Like I love you
No, you don't
It doesn't seem so real anymore
Our clothes all balled up on the floor
We slowly got ourselves dressed
Our hair an amazed flowering mess
I know this isn't the ending at all
You say you're going to find yourself
Well--when you find her,
Come and let me know
I want to see who you really are
I just might be the devil?
You say it's true
I don't want your body anymore
I've had that enough
I want to
Have your soul
I want you to open your mouth and
Have words of truth come out
You're always deep in thoughts, and it keeps you being absurd
But I know what you're thinking without even a word

Your presence is sedated by herbal serenades, medicated
But let me see your wholesome heart elated
You smile at my face, but my glowing eyes see a different you
You're trapped in your life that has done nothing but scare you
Haunted by a ghost of joy
Poisoned by the loss you truly feel
When you're ready to watch it burn,
I'll be there waiting to sweep away the ashes
And I'll pick the last speck of debris off your eyelashes--
Gently pull it away
And blow it into the wind--Like a wish
And I'll embrace you with all the power of the rejected demons
Haunting the ruins of our lives and whisper--Let's go
Is it time to start over?
I am the devil on your shoulder.
I heard when you said, "I'm not miserable."
But I never heard you say,
"I am happy--"

# The Magicians

This insidious death that crept into the spire
of my blood that has led me here
to this realm of shadows
Peeking through the veil to see my beloved one
Seeing the grief on your flesh worn
as if like a badge to signal your chance at change
I'll send you magicians to make but wonderful workings,
turn your water into wine, pour your sadness out into joy--
Send you the witches and shamans to prophecy your future
 Send you the healers and teachers to build up all your knowledge
Send you an angelic host who can defeat the devils
that reside in your homes and hearts
So, you may take off this badge of grief
and sire new clothes for yourself
Grow my sweet child, my love, grow and grow and grow and grow
and heed the signs I've posted on the walls,
in paper leaflets balled up in a drawer,
these artifacts I've left behind
For I am gone, a ghost just hiding now
 here between the shadows
Here just here--watching your light burn, so incredibly bright
So, grow my sweet child, my love, for I will send you magicians--
To water the seeds of your life

# I Just Might be the Devil--Part III

Alone...
Alone...
It's a word I've never liked,
When all that's left is yourself
When you have to put your love away
And take the picture from the shelf
Lay your passion down as if it were
A rotten piece of wealth
I have to say goodbye to you
I have to let you go.
I just might be the devil!
I just might be the devil!!
I just might be the devil!!!!!!!!!!
Destined to be apart from you
--Yearning for your majesty
But I can't see your face crumbling
For what's left of the heart inside me
I will always be there
Just far enough away
To feel your sweet energy
I can watch the crystal fall
And wither like a leaf
From a seed that could've grown into a tree
Maybe one day we'll sit back and laugh

Whether it's as friends
Or as lovers
Or as strangers
And remember what glory we had
Perhaps?
Just a few perfect moments--

# Lonely--

Sitting, standing, pacing, tracing the lines of imaginary people
--Haunting me
Like ghosts of memories
Whispers in the screams of silence
My ears ringing with a word
"What did you say?" Nothing--Warmth of the covers
Not as warm as they could be
Quiet, too quiet
No breathing heavy in the night
Freaks and cracks of the floor
Mice come hither and eat the crumbs I've left
Sneaking from the light in the hall under the door
Nothing--But the scraps of my memories
Thoughts scrubbed down, and sterile
I'm bored like the floorboards nailed in place
Unable to move and some of them screwed
Save me from the void-filled tempest
That perhaps, is my astral projection
Just so I can have some company some self-proclaimed protection
"Well old friend, how've ya been? Where ya been? Where ya goin?"
"I'm lonely," I said to myself.
And myself said, "I know."

# Snow and Rain

You told me about the snow and rain
In January
You told me about the things you lost
In January
You told me that you were healing
But I know you were still in love
With the snow and rain
Do they make you sad?
Do they make you happy?
Do they love you better than I could?
Do they tell you you're beautiful?
Do they dream about you?
He said you wouldn't listen
He said you didn't understand
He knew what would happen
If you ever met his kin
He knew that someday, somehow
That you would fall in love with the
Snow and rain
But rain defeats the snow
And love defeats the sadness
The sunlight breaks them both
For it's the only pure life left to give

# Sayings

If anger is a camera--
photographing what we really are
Then love is the dark room where we develop
and happiness frames any memory we've learned how to cherish
Hang them on the wall.

Clear intent
can be understood by one's magic workings
burning memories and blowing their ashes in the wind.

The only thing water does show us is--
where we leak.

Stare into an empty space long enough and
your mind will see that it is already full.

Cold is the hottest form of apathy
Apathy is the coldest form of empathy.

Love is our conscience choice to be miserable without it.

Silence is the loudest of sounds,
when you're used to hearing everything.

I've put a curse on you.
To see that you're miserable.
But I'm cursed because I'm miserable now too--

I can only think of two things; love and sex.
Unfortunately, the two concepts aren't related.

Simplicity
is a word that drives my mind into
complicated.

# Glue

Big pieces,
Small pieces
Shards of perspective
Lost to the cracks, there
Lost in the floor
I was delicate and glass
And you swung a hammer at me
A hard swing of betrayal
That left me weak
Quite a long wait for the spidering fissures to shatter
In an explosive game of despair, of what does it matter?
It is all your fault
I reflected up at your trust
As you stomped all of the fragments tiny into dust
I swept up the pieces
And I'm taking my time
To place them back together with glue
But a few of the pieces I've left them with you
Stuck in the crevices to the bottom of your boot
I may not be able to fix them all
Missing all the pieces wedged into your shoe
Perhaps tomorrow,
I'll get a little more glue

# Devils will Play

The freezing moon
Burnt silver cold, Black magic spells

Ice fire burning the bones
The demons will rise, and devils will play

# III

# I Wanna Build a Time Machine

# Peter Pan

I never grew up
I'll never get old
My brain didn't mature
Beyond the last star to the left
I'm stern; I'm stoic.
I'm angry all the time
But it's just because
I wanted a little more time
To play--
Imagining me as an explorer
Sailing the oceans wide
A pirate perhaps
Waiting in the tides
For fairies and crocodiles
I waited, for adventures and mummies
And spaceships to the stars
I waited, for love and loss
And giants and kings I waited,
But then I looked in the mirror
And suddenly I saw wrinkles and gray hairs
Where there was once excitement,
I only found sad and lonely stares
And just between
Where you're asleep and awake
In the place where you remember your dreams,
You said you'd be waiting

Well, I wait there too
And someday I'll remember
I can fly and close my eyes
And count to three and remember
All the happiness I'll ever have.
But now I see they've all grown up, and well,
I never had

# Offer

I've burned my dreams
so don't ask about those
and if money doesn't matter
I've got nothing to offer
for I'm the alms for the poor
I have many talents
but none of them are important
I throw away bad emotions
and suffer very little ignorance
I could sing you a song
cook you a meal
tell the greatest stories
that you will ever hear
I could keep you warm through
cold winter nights
and I'll be the first to ask
not, how was your day?
but, how do you feel?
I'll even walk around the house
and turn off all the lights
I'll try to protect you
but I've lost too many fights
I can make you laugh
and I'll hold you when you cry
If you take my offer, I'll stay till we die.

# Room #6

Your hair's a mess, how great a mess?
Your smile is one of satisfactory bliss
I broke into the place in which you hide
I snapped the chains, picked the lock and
Touched the gold and radiant treasure inside
You hid it in a vault of grief
That very few could've opened
The combination perhaps known only to those
Those who were just as lost
I saw you there for the first time
I'll never forget the look
I saw you there for the first time
Here under pressing moonlit blacktop
Smoking drag exhaled desolations,
A touching satisfactory kiss
There I remember
In room, Number 6.

# Hands

All the things we've done my friends
All the things we've touched
Swollen and rusted I feel your grinding
Perhaps a little oil will tender our work?
Struggling to finger the notes on the guitar
The melodies in my head suffered to conjure
Preparing a meal, you burn without heat
The cuisine is still good but my satisfaction has waned
You've caressed all the curves of beautiful bodies
You've built many things and painted as my hobby
But pain is the feeling now related to pleasure
For we cannot have one without the other
I cannot tie my shoes without wincing
And the knots of the noose to dangle
I give up on for leisure
But we continue the journey together
And you cannot escape
You're my tools forever

# Naughty

Protecting your virtues
--all but illusions
You've said, "I'll sell them off no more."
I saw that look
I know what moves you
I've seen those eyes before
If you'd like? I can take you on this floor
You don't want to be sold off
For what was that kind of pleasure
You wanted the "It feels so good!!" kind of roar
You don't want to be "Naughty"
But? The fire feels warm!
Until its flames, they burn you
You're afraid to show love
For fear in the shadows
That--perhaps
It's the only love that's true

# The Price

I would've traversed the heavens
I would've killed any dragon
I would've gone to Tartarus and back
To spend a smile on you
But when I beckoned the gods,
And they summoned a mighty witch of passion
Whose storms have trapped me asunder
Damn it to you, Witch of the Cold Night
I told you this would be the final straw!!
I cannot stop your shivering curse
For, alas even great heroes
Cannot possess the power of gods
As the skies shake away the moans of the lost
I will be found
To spend a smile.

# Parasites

Take the best medicine
And kill all my parasites
They are sucking my life till dry
Anger, and cowardice
Does anything else suffice?
Kill them with the kindest potions
I can find--Worry and Heartache
Eat away at my kidneys
And the pain they inflict is a real disease
Swollen ankles, swollen knees
The signs of the deepest of maladies
It eats and eats and takes and takes
If only it had a name
It does.
It's spelled the same as
L--O--N--E--L--Y
And the medicine that's given of high degree
May only be the real cure for this disease
Perhaps it's spelled the same as L--O--V--E

# Empathy

I see you mister squirrel
Huddling over the warmth of that electrical box.
I see your fears about touching cold snow.
I understand the hunger and worry in your shivers.
You made eye contact with me and I knew.
You know and I know
That the cold storm is coming.
So, hunker down, find your warmth,
And I will do the same.
And when I lay down beside the warmth of slow radiator fire,
I will wonder what has happened to you.
I hope you made it out of the storm alive.
I hope we both knew just how to survive.

# Cold

They say the doors of hell
are locked from the inside.

Well, let me in!!!
It's cold out here.

# Time Machine

I've missed you. Do you miss me?
Can we make it special, one last time?
So, I can remember what we were?
So, I can remember what I'm waiting for ?
Is the hurt too much to bear?
Do I dare go to sleep again
Wondering what I lacked?
Wondering why I wasn't enough?
Wishing to change it all and everything.
Or am I waiting for the end,
The perfect end,
The last goodbye?
The final kiss, the final restraint, the final bliss?
I built a time machine, to change it all,
But I found myself as stubborn to believe,
What would happen if I didn't change?
I could not stop the roaring tide,
For I was then so full of pride.
This love would never end.
So, I snuck in beside you while I was gone
And said my last goodbye.
And made love to you
When you still loved me and
So, it was pure and not filled with lies.
I knew if I changed it, it wouldn't be right.
And the strength I have would have never been.

I never would've finished the time machine
But you don't know. I've already been there--
The perfect end, when I say my last goodbye.
It wasn't in the past, but later on so far away.
I saw us--We were old and gray.
I saw us there at the last goodbye.
The perfect end, as we held our hands together
The final kiss, the last restraint
Death's eternal bliss.

# Solipsism

Flee from truth
Oh! Human animals--too tightly wrapped in a blanket
Soft and warm,
Simple and tight.
It is freedom we have not seen!
But the swatches and samples were right?
How can this be that what I ordered
Wasn't only inconvenient but forever my plight?
I beg of you to roam. Oh! People in the city.
Leave your comforts of the night.
Perhaps freedom is just over the next ridge
Just there out of sight.

# The Hour

How can you enjoy the hour?
If you cannot appreciate the minutes?
Can you even enjoy the seconds?
How do you slow down your thoughts and see?
Every little detail
See its brilliance?
Perhaps when you can, your fears and sorrow melt away.
Perhaps?
The seconds turn to minutes,
    the minutes turn to hours,
    the hours turn to days,
    the days sway to weeks,
    the weeks turn to years,
    the years into eons,
    the eons forever and ever into eternity...

# Red as the Auburn Heart

I remember you from my dreams
I knew you before, didn't I?
A long-lost past wiped clear from our minds at birth
I remember you from my dreams
Red as the auburn sunlight
Red as my auburn heart
Eyes deep penetrating into the very heart of me
I loved you even then
Before the fates drew lots in the sand
Before the shadows told us to fly
Away together farther than the limits of death
Into the bright everlasting, eternal void
Over and over and over, I'd find you
I'll find you--
And two hearts can beat together once again.
I chased your heart through a thousand lifetimes
To find us in a field of red daisies and roses
Running to you--through the empty spaces
To feel the fullness of what
True honest love can be
Patient--Be patient, my love,
I know where to find you.
My heart will always find yours
Beating deep into your breast--
Simple excuses became my motive
Flying through auburn fields of burnt grass

But the flowers of my dreams bloomed
The moment I saw you
A picture--a simple picture
The curves of your face and lines of your eyes
Told me the truth across plains of existence.
Many worlds, many lifetimes,
'Til I found you again.

# The Blue Bone Disease

Walking--Walking until my feet begin to bleed
Shadow men chase me down with shadow dogs
Watching slyly through red-curtained windows
Video electric eyeballs documenting my every move
Wondering what it was that I had lost
I only wish to see the water again, one last time
Before I go away far too far--away for good
Walking--Walking until my feet begin to bleed
Bones crunching on bones, knee to bone, bone to soft mass
You'll never catch me slipping, I whisper to myself
I won't be enticed by your traps
Why would they do this to me? I thought I was good?
Why such tricks would be had on my mind--My memories?
It was real? This is real. THIS IS REAL!
WHY WOULD YOU DO THIS TO ME?
Keep walking--Walking until my feet begin to bleed
Snowblind soldiers armed in the woods,
Hiding just there, like tigers
I can see you. I see you.
Tactical rifles aimed to capture me. Why?
Was the poison in my bones made for me? To see?
Was this a big game? Was this the one that I was to win?
Perhaps I was meant to lose--
Oh, Devil in this wilderness, tempt me no more!
Walking--Walking until my feet begin to bleed
There must be only one destination
One special home for me; I'm headed down
Deep into the cold waters, never to return

The empty cold darkness--
How could you be so cruel to me?
How could you do this to me?
My bones are filled deep with the deepest blues
Easily broken, brittle spires and stems
It's a sadness, a sickening disease
Being alive
A shriek, a thousand birds, swarming above my head
Beckoning lost futures; traded for fear and ignorance
But like a seam of golden thread, the first beams of light
peek over the water
Shooting me upward to peer wildly into the sky
The empty black sky broke
Blinding, shutting, wincing, and searing
The backs of the orbs
I cannot see; I'm ready with my shame
Oh! beaming God of Light, magnificent bringer of warmth,
I'm ready now
I'm ready
I'm ready
Walking--Walking until my feet begin to bleed
The journey's just begun; it never ended
It only brightened--

# The End #2

I cannot see the end
Not because it is far
But because it is too beautiful to look at
I cannot see the path
Not because it is hidden
But because I have no one to show me the way
So maybe, just maybe,
Can I make a path of my own?
Perhaps show myself the way?
For I know the end is bright
And it's oh, so beautiful
But it would be nice
To have some company
On this journey to find this glorious end
It's not because I need you
It's not because I want you
It's because I know you will be there
Would you like to see the end with me?

# Sunflowers and Sage

Perhaps loving glares
And simply smiling stares
Are exactly as they appear
I don't want to ruin the moment
With my words, so, I say nothing
But hurting hearts
And our defective parts
Wired up in our sacred scars
Leave us speechless
I don't want to ruin the moment
With the lines on my face, so, I say nothing
But I see the truth in your sunflower eyes
Turned to fire red in the darkness
Made alive by the prismatic light
Turned as green as the sacred sage
That cleanses the demons that live inside
It's the broken ones that need it the most
The shimmering sunlight that two people can share
In primitive moments showing how much we can care
Let me turn your sunflowers to sage and
Let me clean off the past performance from the stage
I don't want to ruin the moment
With my words, so, I say nothing
But love is so easily written down
In a note perhaps, but it's as easy as planting seeds
The feelings so easily written--down on the page.

# IV

# I Wanna be an Astronaut

# The Bloody Flag

Raise high the bloody flag!
Raise home the idea of taking back your wealth
Like in madness, moving the center of the universe
From the earth below
To the bright sun beyond
To the empty blackness that galactic swaths empty
That not even time so dear can escape its pain.
The realms of belief fear all that the gods have been executed.
Disemboweled by the electric palm readers
The emptiness of fulfillment
Knowledge begins and ends with experience
Truth is as arbitrary as use of the mechanical
to mend the biological
Sinew can bind flesh together
But cannot mend glitches in the mind
Philos replaced by psyche.
Faith replaced by science.
How great!
Raise the Bloody flag!
Kill what is red and blue
Kill what is dying
With what is new
Oh, enslaved to commerce!
ME--OH, lowly SERVANT!
Work for your pennies
Work for your paper
I'll work for my liberty
The construction of the mind

Trade my comfort for freedom.
Landless and mindless, obedience outweighs
Enlightened thinking
Manufacture what is meant for the trash
Manufacture what is meant to control
Never mind our mother
Never mind nature
It's garbage on the sides of your roads
Thoroughfares you don't have to walk through
Binding sludge stuck to my heart
*Raise high the bloody flag!*
I am a pirate to steal back that which I do not own
The most valuable gold
The shining value of my mind
It is forever mine.
So hang me if you have to.
As a pirate, I will be condemned to death
My gold, my own, the gold between my ears.
BEHOLD--It was carved in scars
YOUR GODS ARE DEAD
MY EARTH IS DYING
RAISE IT HIGH, THE BLOODY FLAG!!!
Take back what is yours to own
For your end is owned by death alone.
Only he can grant your final liberty.

# What I Imagined

## *The Plague*

This is not the world I imagined.
My poor people pushed six feet apart
Fear in our breath, Fear on our faces
Our covered identities
Our covered emotions
There are too many dead, their ashes in vain
Divided we are, cracked apart,
We should all be ashamed
We should have been brought together
This is not the world I imagined
I don't mind being imprisoned
Chained and locked from the inside
For me to set my OWN confinements
Is It? "For my health?"
People shouting, "It's a lie!"
While hordes of fellow humans die
People retort at the sight of me,
Why are you afraid?
YOU are SUPPOSED TO BE MY family
Oh me? I'm not sick--But, you could be.

# With You Soon

I see you, little boy playing with imaginary toys
Don't grow up too fast, and don't make too much noise
It seems like such a long time gone, but if you listen real close
You will hear a pretty song
And I will sing you a sweet little tune
Daddy will be with you soon
I know it isn't fair
It isn't much better for me
The wind you know it does decree
That every minute hurts
Every second is a winch to my heart
But those who love you don't seem to care
I hope that they didn't tell you
That Daddy, well, he's just a little sick
That's just a little trick
That those who love you want to spin so they
Don't have to share the time
Cuz' the truth is, my boy
That Daddy, he is doing just fine
So, sing my boy a sweet little tune
Daddy will be with you soon

# Don't Worry 'Bout Anything

It's not your fault
It's not that I've changed
But something isn't right in here without you
I'm too old, to not know who I am
But, it's not done
It's not fun
Only things I know
Only things I see
Falling down on me
You said, "I don't care."
But you couldn't be more wrong
But I don't know how to live anymore
It's quiet
I'd prefer to not say a word
I'd prefer to bury myself down deep
So, I can hide
Don't you worry about anything
Cuz' it will go away
It will go away

# Astronaut

"Mom, when I grow up
I'm gonna be an astronaut
I'm gonna fly higher than anyone else
I'm gonna make my home in the stars."

"Mom, when I grow up
I'm gonna be a rock and roll star
I'm gonna be louder than anyone else
I'm definitely gonna be a star
Everyone will love me. I'll be living large."

"Mom, when I grow up
I'm gonna be unemployed
I'm only gonna be worth my work
I'm gonna get higher than anyone else
I'm gonna find solace in bottles and pills
I'm gonna find comfort in needles and girls."

"Mom, when I grow up
I'll still be me
I'll still find love
I'll still find my way to the stars."
"Mom, when I grow up
I'm gonna be an astronaut."

# My Little Room

Tie them together, the lines, the corners,
of my little room
Everything in its place, neatly ordered,
placed with care
Everything a color, everything alive
The windows allow the light to move
Shining bright upon my bed,
The smells of incense and tobacco
My guitar gently sitting in the corner,
put away like a dunce child
Waiting for the time to play
My towel hanging over the warm radiator
Ready to dry and clean at a moment's notice
I am the master of my little room.
Nothing moves without my direction
Nothing gains its freedom,
Its will is under my control.
I am the Lord here
My things are my servants.
I am King of this nowhere,
King of the four square
The game I play here, in my little room
Until the door opens and I let in the gloom
But for now, I am safe in my little room.

# Headache #3

--Blisters to my spine
--Fire in my eyes
--Wheezing: "I can't breathe."
My chest caving in--
My legs shattering into sand
Why is my skin melting away?
Dissolving into relief--Sweet relief.

# 61st

The police drive slowly down the cross-street
Looking for the guilty, who occupy every apartment.
Coming and going and leaving.
I see them all moving about like rats.
"Give me the money," "Where are my goods?"
What's good? The Goods.
I walk slowly to the corner store, and I hear a yell.
"Hey, Lemme get a cigarette!" You can't afford them?
Neither can I.
What do I do to keep a clean soul?
Among the sinners in droves who look me in the eyes
And tell me "You're strange."
But isn't the fact that I'm different,
The pressure cooker of change?
Or perhaps I'm feeling old.
But I am not unlike you.
I am the sinner, above in his nest. Waiting.
I've been you; I will be you again.
A monster. Grotesque.
But I sit above now, in this room
Watching the corner of the street.
Having been you, having seen you,
Having NOW *not* been you.
What am I then? One of the guilty?
NO. Just the watcher of the street.

# Mini-blinds

The blood spray on the mini-blinds
I know what happened in this room
Some time ago, it was never wiped away
The little dots have grown mold and gathered dust
But the wound does seem fresh to me
The iron has faded to rust, but the hole it left, deep in my arms
Has never faded from me
Never faded from my tempered steel vessels
Even when the bruises have gone
I've seen this scene before in a gas station bathroom
However, never where I have to sleep
I don't know who did it
But thank you for the reminder

# Retaliation

You hurt me
So I hurt you
You don't care
So why should I?
"Life is too short"
As a battle cry
{Dies in despair of heavy sighs}
Waste of time
Don't you love me?
/Why should I?\
Because you can
Because it's right
So, stab me deep
Deep in the mess
Deep in the guts
Eviscerate me
-Make it hurt-
-Call it just-
(Call it what
you want to)
"Retaliation"
"I will"
"ok"
"!"

# None

Sterile blue and Sterile blue
Cold and Blue
Repetition is the name I give
the experience of exile--
You forget the words--
You forget your name--
The words sound foreign to me now
Every syllable of my name no longer
feels like an ID-entity
A string of thoughts and impulses
You wake, you move, but none
of it has any nuance, substance
Apathy is an excuse
Rage is what bubbles--(sic)
Like glycerin forming domes ready to explode
But the whimpering sound of a puppy
is the sanctioned emotion
Tell them how you really feel
and they say you have no right
Ha! To take my own life?
I have nothing to say,
"But who gave you this right?"
So, we drink to feel numb.
We fuck to feel cum.
We end it all to feel none.

# Good on You

"No Justice, No Peace"
Reigns, riots in the streets
If you're worried about the looting,
are you missing the point?
and that's why they're shooting?
Our taxes pay the salary
of murderers and oppressors
And a rivalry of hate
passed down by successor
The press and president
calling us hurting, Thugs.
What are we supposed to do,
end tyranny with hugs?
We're supposed to be
"Non-violent peaceful protestors."
Well, that's what the
armor-clad warriors expect
Tear gas clouds bring rain
of tears to the repressors
When they would have no
problem bringing you death
While setting a fire to the
businesses and precinct
In hopes that this will end another generation of hate
In hopes that this conspiracy of safety will go extinct
Good on you America.

We ended a quarantine,
to start a revolution.
There're 100,000 dead.
All of us coping with the trauma.
And that doesn't bother you, does it?
Can't we go back to start making money?
Good on you America. We kill our own
innocents and burn down the streets
George Floyd is dead. Calling out "MOMMA."
And that doesn't bother you, does it?
You People don't care. You say,
"You're just stalling the economy."
Hearts hurt for all who have died,
and we know that things need to change
Can't we come together and face all of this?
For we know these times, they are strange
But don't bury your heads and condemn
all whom you pity
With --"NO JUSTICE, NO PEACE."
Fires still blaze in the Twin Cities

# Ruby Lips

She comes strong like the light
You know her desire seems right
With her grace, she moves in like a vampire
Takes everything I give her and more
I wanna take you home tonight
"Baby, only if you show me a sign." Show me tonight
You know that something ain't just right
But, you take me down with your ruby lips
O-o-o-o-h, your ruby lips
You take my heart and make it skip
Your eyes so big, your moonlight drips
I love your way and it keeps me torn--
Her beauty makes you wish you'd never been born
Speaking with magic of the tides
The only thing I'm holding inside
Like a spirit whispers out loud and it cries
To a hope intended for the absence denied

# Gyandomorphism

Pain of being two things
Life before traction
The level of screaming feedback
Holding the bell until it ends its ring
Putting on your pretty face
Despite your inclination not to
When you don't, they say you're a disgrace
But that is something they'll have to prove
For in my dominion
I'm the one to move
It isn't fact or opinion
In fact, it's facts you have to prove
They will take my spirit and my mate
And they won't even call it rape
But when they see the pain in my gait
They will know that I am just disgraced
Half of one and half the other
In love with both
But not the other

# Burn

Branded by the sheer size of work
Hurt by a simple task
Three days of fire on the skin
A silent smear of melted flesh
Left me scarred on the right arm
Working till my bones ache from stress
Bending fractures in my calves
Blisters on my feet
Blisters on my skin
A callous from the knife
I hold in my hand
Everything's done.
"Knife Is Life"
is graffiti on the side of the fridge
The week is over. To do it again--
Satisfaction
--Is the "choice" adjective
What a flavor left on my tongue

## About the Author:

Born on the 28th of November, 1986 in a suburb of Chicago,
**Michael M. Mehlan** is a musician, artist, poet, and loving father of one.
He currently lives in Cicero, IN.
He has previously written under the pen name of *Jolly Jackson.*

His music is available at: https://jollyjackson.bandcamp.com/

*Matthew D. Mehlan*

www.ingramcontent.com/pod-product-compliance
Lightning Source LLC
Chambersburg PA
CBHW060535130626
46553CB00002B/766